D1292779

What Happens in Winter?

# Plants in Winter

by Jenny Fretland VanVoorst

Bullfrog Books

# Ideas for Parents and Teachers

Bullfrog Books let children practice reading informational text at the earliest reading levels. Repetition, familiar words, and photo labels support early readers.

### Before Reading

- Discuss the cover photo. What does it tell them?

- Look at the picture glossary together. Read and discuss the words.

### Read the Book

- "Walk" through the book and look at the photos. Let the child ask questions. Point out the photo labels.

- Read the book to the child, or have him or her read independently.

### After Reading

- Prompt the child to think more. Ask: What kinds of plants do you have where you live? What happens to them in the wintertime?

Bullfrog Books are published by Jump!
5357 Penn Avenue South
Minneapolis, MN 55419
www.jumplibrary.com

Library of Congress Cataloging-in-Publication Data

Names: Fretland VanVoorst, Jenny, 1972– author.
Title: Plants in winter / by Jenny Fretland VanVoorst.
Description: Minneapolis, MN: Jump!, Inc. [2017]
Series: Bullfrog books. What happens in winter?
Audience: Ages 5–8. | Audience: K to grade 3.
Includes index.
Identifiers: LCCN 2016005398 (print)
LCCN 2016006047 (ebook)
ISBN 9781620313954 (hardcover: alk. paper)
ISBN 9781620314999 (paperback)
ISBN 9781624964428 (ebook)
Subjects: LCSH:
Plants in winter—Juvenile literature.
Winter—Juvenile literature.
Classification:
LCC SB439.5.F74 2017 (print)
LCC SB439.5 (ebook) | DDC 581.4/3—dc23
LC record available at http://lccn.loc.gov/2016005398

Series Designer: Ellen Huber
Book Designer: Leah Sanders
Photo Researcher: Amy Gensmer

Photo Credits: All photos by Shutterstock except: Dreamstime, 8–9; Getty Images, 5.

Printed in the United States of America at Corporate Graphics in North Mankato, Minnesota.

# Table of Contents

# Time to Rest

Winter is here.

The ground freezes.
Water freezes.

There is less sun.

It is time for
plants to rest.

Flowers stop growing.

# Grass stops growing.

**Crops stop growing, too.**

11

Some trees dropped
their leaves in the fall.

Why?

Leaves make
food for trees.

But in winter
the trees do not
make food.

The leaves dried up.
They fell off.
Now the branches
are bare.

# Evergreens keep their needles.

needle

18

They stay green through the winter.

Soon the weather will warm.

Plants will grow again.

Look for the crocus.

It is a sign that spring is coming.

# Trees in Winter

Some trees have needles instead of leaves. They don't drop their needles when the weather gets cold. They stay green all winter.

Some trees, such as oaks and maples, drop their leaves in the fall. The branches are bare all winter. Leaves grow again in the spring.

# Picture Glossary

**crocus**
A flowering plant that is one of the first to bloom in the spring.

**evergreens**
Having leaves that remain green through several growing seasons.

**crops**
Plants or plant products that can be grown and harvested.

**needles**
Long, slender leaves shaped like a needle; pine trees have needles.

# Index

# To Learn More

Learning more is as easy as 1, 2, 3.

1) Go to www.factsurfer.com

2) Enter "plantsinwinter" into the search box.

3) Click the "Surf" button to see a list of websites.

With factsurfer.com, finding more information is just a click away.

24